ACROSS THE BRIDGE

"A QUEER, ANTI-SUICIDE/PRO-LIVING COMING-OF-AGE STORY"

by Michael Simones
Illustrated by Eminence System

This book may be purchased by contacting the publisher and author (wcrowspub@gmail.com).

Publisher: White Crow S-Publishing

ISBN-979-8-9877310-2-4 (softcover)
ISBN-979-8-9877310-3-1 (hardcover)
Library of Congress Control Number: 2024909725

Printed in the U.S.A

ACKNOWLEDGEMENTS

First, I want to thank God for showing me that there is a higher power that loves their LGBTQIA+ children, youth and adults. You will read about this later in the story.

I want to thank my mom who made the deal with me as a teenager and young adult that if I make the decision to drink, that I will not drive, and if I have to for safety reasons, to call her and she would pick me up with no questions asked. She wanted me to be alive over getting mad. I had to use this two times in my youth and she kept her promise.

I want to thank all of the US Air Force officers who, during my career, broke through personal and political feelings in order to seek my advise about queer youth issues, in order to set the right course for families.

I want to thank the San Francisco establishments at which I do all of my writing: Starbucks and Capitol One Cafe. They see me almost everyday and are so kind to me. This helps so much with the writing process.

DISCLAIMER

This book contains storylines related to underage (teen) drinking and marijuana use. As an adult, I in no way condone this behavior, however it can happen whether parents like it or not. I highly recommend parental education on alcohol and marijuana use!

There are also storylines related to bisexuality, transgender awareness and descriptive male with male teen intimacy.

There is a storyline related to self-harm and suicidal thoughts and actions.

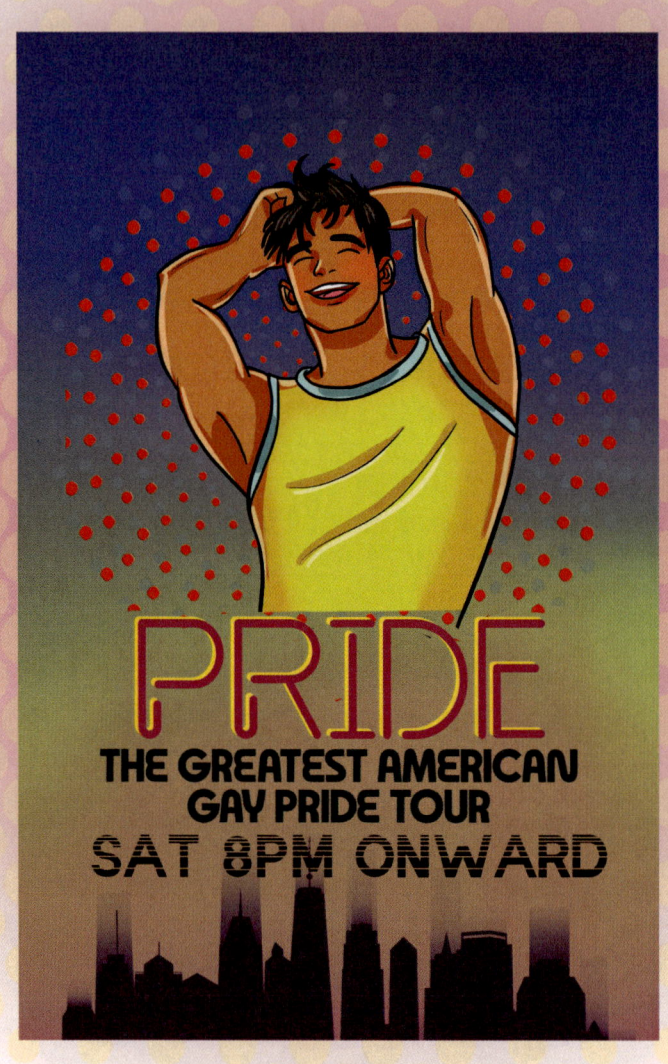

DEDICATION

This graphic novel is dedicated to all of the queer youth that have died because our society did not openly embrace them for who they are. They were never mentored into removing themselves from the negative environment and therefore finding a place where they can thrive as an LGBTQIA+ person.

We love you and will always remember you!

A part of their legacy is the reminder that we *must* preserve our queer history, tell our individual stories and educate the next generation and generations to come that we are here. We are great people and we must eradicate queer suicides ignited by unbridled religions and a severe lack of public education.

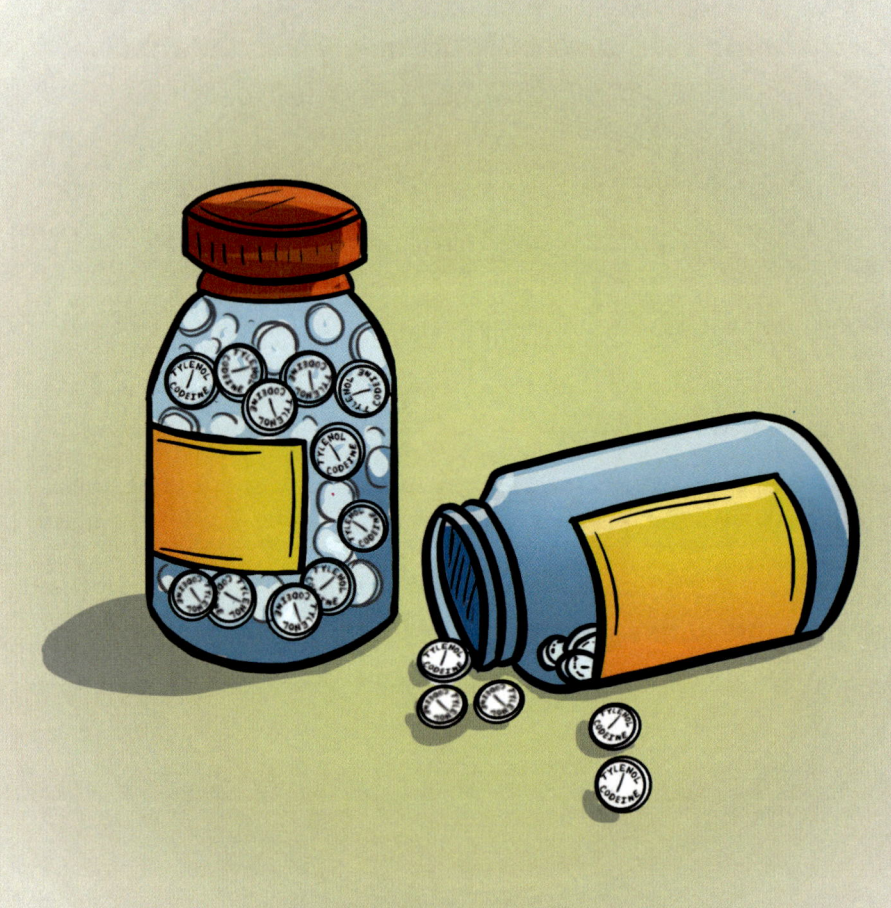

A MESSAGE FROM THE AUTHOR

This is a story of how a young person called Ryder came to terms with and embraced his queerness, and the path he took to overcome small-town homophobia and to eventually place himself in an environment where he could be himself and thrive.

I want all young queer people to know that oppressive shame for being queer (that is what oppressors want) can be overcome and acts of self-harm need to be eradicated.

Ryder personally chose to overcome oppression and shame and it was the best decision he ever made. It paved the way to an amazing career and life as a queer male!

Please don't be put off by the fact that this story is set in the 1980s. As long as our society promotes homophobia and transphobia and tries to inflict shame on us, so that we will either stay in the closet or become someone we are not, this story unfortunately remains relevant in any decade. Also, I think you'll love the 80s references!

Michael Simones (he/him/his)
USAF-CIV (ret.)/Author

WORDS & DEFINITIONS

queer phobia:
hatred directed towards the members of the LGBTQIA+ community as a whole

transphobia:
hatred directed towards the transgender community

homophobia:
hatred directed towards people that identify as lesbian, gay or bisexual

heteronormative:
denoting or relating to a world view that promotes heterosexuality as the normal or preferred sexual orientation

non-binary:
someone who does not identify as exclusively a man or a woman

gender non-conforming:
behavior or gender expression by an individual that does not match masculine or feminine gender norms

LGBTQIA+ FRIENDLY HOTLINES

The Trevor Project
(www.thetrevorproject.org)
1-866-488-7386

LGBT National Hotline
1-888-843-4564

COMING OUT SUPPORT

Human Rights Campaign (www.hrc.org)

TABLE OF CONTENTS

CHAPTER 1
The Favor

HELLO! My name is Ryder and I am queer.

I didn't realize this until my senior year of high school. I spent the first three years with feelings of being different—but I didn't understand them. What I did know was that when other boys talked about girls and how they wanted to have sex with them, I didn't get it or feel anything. What did come naturally for me was noticing cute guys. I enjoyed that! That was the extent of my queerness at that point.

Then, in September of my senior year...like an earthquake! Out of the blue. Everything changed. And I mean, everything! From knowing who I was sexually, to my social life and thinking about life after high school—it all changed. And here is what happened.

I was sitting in my fourth-period English class, the first to arrive. The class before mine was sophomore English, and some of the students stayed behind to talk with the teacher. Then, wow! This really hot sophomore came up to me, sat down and said in a hurried voice, "You're Ryder right?" My heart was racing!

Okay, before I get to how I responded, I have to explain just how hot this sophomore was. To me he looked Italian, but later I found out he was half Hispanic and half Caucasian. He had beautiful skin that made my heart melt. He was about 5'11" tall, thick dark brown hair and a smile that for the first time in my life caught my attention at a different level.

When he spoke to me I was so scared to say the wrong thing or do something wrong. I had never felt this way before. I had no idea that this boy was about to change my life—forever!

"Yeah," I responded, trying so hard not to show my attraction.

"I'm Nate," he said. "I know your cousin Troye; he's a friend of my brother's."

"Oh, okay."

"Hey, I gotta go," he said, "but can I meet you here tomorrow? I have something I want to ask you."

I felt such relief that I'd see him again, and that we'd even get to talk. "Yeah no problem!" I said.

This was without a doubt the beginning of my first crush!

We lived in a small rural town, and before I go on with the story, I really need to let you know what "small town USA" was like back then. Then I'll get to "the favor"—I promise!

I attended high school in the late 70s-early 80s. At the time, the population of the town was around 2500-3000 people. It's a rural community, which is nice in itself, however if you have no interest in agriculture or in playing sports, you're automatically considered weird and your social status is low.

At the time, the population was mostly Caucasian. There was one Black family, considered to be of lower social status, who did odd jobs to financially survive. There was a larger Mexican population, in the same economic status as the Black family, however, unlike the Black children, in school the Mexicans were segregated from the White children. The state's reasoning for this at the time was that they were ESL (English As A Second Language) students and this required special education. This policy ran from elementary school to high school when I was growing up.

When it came to religion, the majority of the population was Catholic or Christian-based, so bearing in mind what I've already told you, you can imagine attitudes towards homosexuality, bisexuality and being gender non-conforming!

When you're an LGBTQIA+ child in elementary school, you begin to know that you're different, but you don't understand it. Some people, like me, don't understand it even in high school. However, regardless of age, constantly having to listen to the negative and derogatory comments about LGBTQIA+ people from parents, family members, family friends and others instills a message that being queer is a bad thing, and that the community condones and supports the poor treatment of queer people. The queer phobia, homophobia and transphobia level in this small town was high!

When I was in high school, a teen from a nearby town was killed by a car while walking on a remote country road. The authorities certified the case as a car accident. But a couple years later, I learned from some older LGBTQIA+ people that it was a gay bashing that had been covered up. The teen had been to a queer party and was ambushed by a car full of homophobic teens when walking home. The driver said it was an accident, and that was that.

This gives you an idea as to the environment that I and the rest of the characters in this story lived in at the time.

Don't get me wrong, I was raised by a loving family and relatives, however, they carried with them generational, geographic and institutionalized queer phobia. It was not only present, it was verbalized often and was hurtful to listen to growing up.

As for my existence as an LGBTQIA+ child/teen in this small town, I survived. And for the most part I kept happy by being invisible. I chose to stay in the background socially. I didn't attend any dances or proms. I just couldn't fake it. I had no desire to dance with girls or to be part of the boy-girl rituals. They just had a hollow meaning to me. I was very content noticing cute guys though!

No matter the oppression level, we LGBTQIA+ teens (and allies) in this small rural community seemed to find each other. However, being closeted was critical. There was no support for being queer.

Now that you have a clear picture of the rural community this is set in, I can get to the favor.

As planned, Nate and I met between classes the next day. With this being my first heavy crush, you can imagine that I didn't get much sleep the night before!

Nate slipped me a note (there were no mobile phones or email back then) that said, *Please if you can call me—can you get me a bottle of clc (Canadian Whiskey)?* Nate. He included his phone number.

Fuck! This really hot sophomore was asking me to do something that was totally wrong! But he was so cute and I had such a crush on him. I wanted to make him happy, but I didn't want to break the law. Even though we were minors, I was guessing it was still illegal. He must have thought it was easy for me to do since my family owned a restaurant and bar.

Well, like most queer teens experiencing a serious crush for the first time, guess which side won!

I did it! I snuck an almost full bottle from my parents' cabinet.

I know it was wrong, but a first-time queer crush makes you do things that you normally wouldn't.

I called Nate that night and let him know I had his bottle. We made plans for him to pick it up on Saturday afternoon— he was getting together with a couple of his friends at one of their homes.

That afternoon went to plan, and what remained after was a connection. I didn't even know if he was queer. I thought so—I hoped so—but wasn't sure. All I knew was that even though I'd done something wrong, it connected us in a way I'd never imagined, and I'd meet new LGBTQIA+ friends and allies! "The favor" was the beginning of my queer life!

   Nate and I never met up at school, mainly because we were in different grades and social circles. That was okay, because at night we would talk on the phone for about two hours. We each had our own phone in our rooms, so we could talk with privacy. We mainly just got to know each other—likes, dislikes and gossip about kids at school and teachers. We talked about our families and cracked a lot of jokes. Nate was a comedian! He could make a joke about anything, which made things fun and we laughed a lot.

After a couple weeks of fun phone conversations, we met up. I had a car—a 1979 Pontiac Trans AM—so we would cruise around our town and just chat and laugh. This was a hot car in the early 80s, and there was a TV show aired later in the 80s called *Night Rider* that made it even more famous. That car was my pride and joy, and it became a meeting point for me and Nate's friends who I'd meet later on.

One of our favorite stops was the famous 80s records and tapes store, Tower Records. Nate introduced me to the world of heavy metal, and top of our list was AC/DC. This band later became our friend group's go-to music, and was a permanent fixture in the Trans AM's cassette player.

Our nightly phone calls, and cruising in the Trans AM, went on for a couple weeks, and then came a second favor. This one came with an invitation, and I said yes.

CHAPTER 2

The Group Forms

Nate asked me for another bottle of whiskey from my parents stash, and this time invited me to join his friends. A senior, one junior and five sophomores. What a combination! There were others that came in and out of our partying, but this was our core friends group:

I didn't know anything about them before we started partying. Apart from Aiden, who was an extremely good-looking athlete and was therefore well known.

The funny thing was, they were almost all part of the popular scene in school in their grade.

This friend group was actually a subgroup, separate from daily high school life, and I later learned why.

I want to describe to you the party scene when we were all together. There were three variations: at someone's house when families were away; cruising in my Trans AM, and *The Rocky Horror Picture Show*. (Note: if you've never seen the movie musical *The Rocky Horror Picture Show*, I highly recommend that you do. It will really help you understand the rest of the story.)

We mostly met at Kenji's house when his family was out. My house was second to be used, when my parents were on a trip and sister was staying with one of her friends.

Our soundtrack was either AC/DC blaring on the cassette player, or the top 40 playing on the local radio station (a mixture of pop and rock). There was always pot and alcohol.

After the second favor, I wasn't asked to bring anything else again, so I'm not sure where it all came from, but it was there—from vodka to whiskey. The pot was a signature feature, as much as the alcohol and AC/DC. I don't know where that came from either, but pot wasn't my thing so I didn't ask questions.

I was the only one over 16 and with a car, so I stayed sober because the house parties sometimes moved on to cruising in the Trans AM.

As you'll know by now, these were my first real experiences of teen parties. The vibe made me feel so welcome, in spite of the age difference. An unspoken feeling of individual and sexual freedom instantly hooked me into it all. Sure, the pot and alcohol played their part, but it was more than that. It was the touching, sitting close and sometimes on top of each other, no matter what gender. There was an innocent flirting between "some" of the guys—no words, just vibes. It was a subgroup of people just being themselves, away from the school politics, gender expectations and societal phobias. It was a group of teens unconsciously escaping the small-mindedness of a small rural town into something that was more naturally human.

Now that I've described the group as a whole, I want to tell you about each person in the group, and more about myself and Nate.

Let's start with the only girl in the group—Maya. She was very popular in school; quiet, and got great grades. When she was with us in the subgroup she was what I'd call a "quiet wild." She loved to move to pop music when she was stoned, or drinking.

Maya and Kenji were a thing. The two were pretty inseparable when we were all together—usually making out towards the end of a party.

Her favorite part in the *Rocky Horror* film was the scene between Magenta and Columbia when they sang "Touch-A Touch-A Touch Me—I want to be Dirty", which she often acted out with her friend Melissa. Magenta and Columbia were her favorite characters in the movie.

Maya was such a nice person. She would do anything for anyone. She was also a good listener and became the go-to person for all of us if we needed to vent about a problem. You could confide in her.

Then there was Kenji—the most admired in the group. Kenji was Nate's best friend and Kenji's biggest fan! Why? He is just so cool in everything he did, from good looks to personality. A good guy all around with a kind heart, like Maya.

In school Kenji was popular, quiet, average grades and everyone's friend. A modern, clean-cut dresser, which added to his good looks.

Kenji was great with mechanics and the 80s technology. It was he who worked on the Trans AM, installing the cassette player and other extras that I bought for the car. Installing things wasn't my thing, but Kenji was great at it.

In the subgroup he was another quiet crazy. Loved being stoned; would crank up the AC/DC and play over and over (which we all liked) and make out with Maya.

His favorite character in *Rocky Horror* was Riff Raff. It kind of made sense—Riff Raff, like Kenji, was the quiet storm of the movie, as Kenji was to our group.

So who was the loud voice of the group? Nate. He was the loud voice and the leader; the party and cruising planner. It was Nate who made sure there was alcohol or pot or both and that everyone was having fun. He was the life of the party. Without Nate, there would have been no first queer crush for me, no subgroup and no fun!

In school Nate got average grades, and was popular because he was funny and on the football team—although he didn't seem to take playing football that seriously. His passion was more about our subgroup, and it was him who introduced us to *The Rocky Horror Picture Show*. His favorite character was Frank-N-Furter.

Nate wasn't in a relationship, but there was a lot of talk about his one-off sexual encounters with girls in his class—I don't know how true it was, or if it was a cover up. More about this later.

He was very loud when stoned or drunk, dancing around and always a comedian. He wasn't one to sit still for any length of time. When the rest of us were having fun being laid back, listening to AC/DC and hanging off each other, Nate was up and keeping things alive. He always made sure we were all having fun.

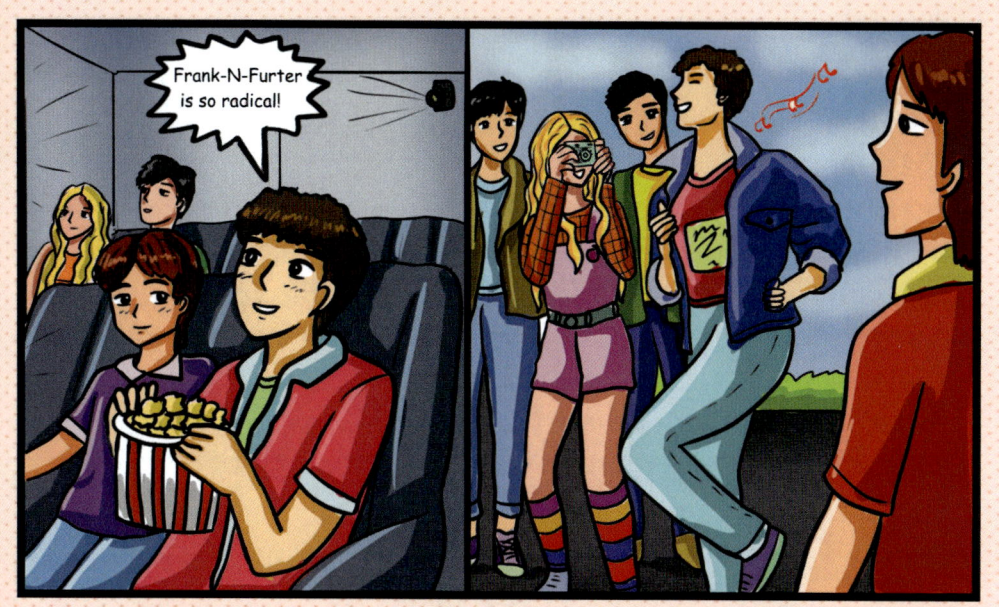

As much as I was crushing on Nate and would do anything for him (obviously—look what I'd done so far) there was a scary side to him.

Nate loved to flirt with unsafe and possibly fatal situations. It scared Maya and me a lot, but didn't seem to phase the rest of the group. Shoplifting was the lightest of the scary stuff. On numerous occasions we'd separate at the mall or some shopping place, only to get back to the Trans AM to find him with one or more stolen items. I didn't like it, but when you are crushing on someone, you tend to focus on the positive rather than the negative. I think most of you will know what I mean!

Another issue was getting pot from guys who were way older than us and who to me looked shady and criminal. In one incident Nate bought a couple joints that were obviously laced with something else stronger, and we all thought we were going to die.

Scariest of all was when he risked serious injury, or even death. It was bad enough when he did this to himself, but it was something else when he did it to his friends. The others in the subgroup would laugh it off, but I guess since I was older, or maybe just because of my personality, I was scared and hated it.

To give you a couple of examples, there were these mountains we'd drive up to from time to time, just to chill. Nate would stand on the edge of the cliff and pretend to fall. One other time we took my dad's dune buggy out to these same mountains and Nate would grab the steering wheel when I was driving and veer it so we'd head straight for the edge of the mountain. Very scary! The reason I'm sharing this side of Nate with you is because it becomes a big part of the story later. Don't get me wrong, Nate was a great guy. He just had this dark side that worried me—a lot!

The most popular person in the group was the only junior—Aiden. Perfect grades; on every sports team past and present (and his body showed it), and popular at school, too, not only among juniors. At first I was puzzled as to why Aiden was a part of this group, but as I got to know him, it became clear to me that his popularity and perfect grades were draining for him. The subgroup was a way to escape—

as it was for all of us, but for different reasons.

In the group Aiden was kind of quiet, but what made him stand out was his way he always had to have parts of his body showing. He had a hot body, and he knew it and liked to show it off. It was hot for me to watch—obviously. He was famous for sitting close to any of us with his shirt open or his gym shorts revealing just a little too much. He was another great guy that just happened to love his physique and show it off too. I didn't mind!

Aiden had a girlfriend at the time, but she never came to any of our parties or cruising or even to see *Rocky Horror*. I didn't think anything of it at the time, but later it came to me that even though he liked her, she was a part of the exhausting heteronormative world. He didn't want the two worlds to merge. All of us kind of felt the same way.

What a surprise! Aiden's favorite character in *Rocky Horror* was Rocky.

Luke and Christian joined our subgroup about a month after the rest of us started hanging out. Both were not so popular in school and got average grades, but they too were looking for a place in our small town and in teen society in which they could be themselves. Initially friends of Kenji, they ended up fitting in very well.

Both loved to get wasted and to just chill. Luke was more of what I'd call a public flirt, while Christian was more one on one and private in his flirting. Neither was in a relationship, but it was very clear to me that Christian had a crush on Kenji—yes, straight Kenji.

Luke was a very nervous, can't-sit-still type of person. He would get loud at times and annoy the hell out of Maya, but he was harmless. He often flirted with me and would sit close to me—which I loved because of the boy-to-boy contact.

Luke's favorite characters in *Rocky Horror* were Brad and Eddie and Christian's was Rocky.

We were together pretty much every Friday night, and on Saturdays, either day or night or both. We would party at someone's house, cruise around town in the Trans AM with our favorite heavy metal music blaring, and go almost every Saturday night to the midnight showing of *The Rocky Horror Picture Show.*

Kenji would get the car ready before we left, and cruising would start with getting stoned—everyone except me, because I was the only driver. That was okay, because I didn't like pot anyway. We would cruise around feeling cool in the Trans AM, stopping at drive-through fast-food places— our favorite was *Carl's Jr.* On our way home from the movie we'd play the *Rocky Horror* soundtrack.

We liked to stop at Tower Records; would maybe even buy something if we had extra cash. And we'd go to the local smoke shop (a store that sells marijuana paraphernalia) and look at bongs, etc. This all lasted for two to three hours.

We laughed a lot for obvious reasons (pot), but mostly felt young and alive, especially with the T-top of the car removed.

Before I met Nate, I'd never even heard of *The Rocky Horror Picture Show*. Little did I know the impact that it would have on my young queer life, and for everyone in the group. There was no greater influence on me and my friends. The movie played every Saturday night in a theatre about 50 minutes away from our town, and was the second of a double feature. The first movie started at 10pm, and *Rocky* started at midnight.

REMINDER: If you've never seen the movie/musical *The Rocky Horror Picture Show*, I highly recommend that you do. It will help so much on understanding the rest of the story.

It's messy—you can dress up like the characters, bring props to throw, and act out scenes, while adding funny comments to the show. (At the time of publication, YouTube has several videos and commentaries on the way to participate in the show. There are also books available.)

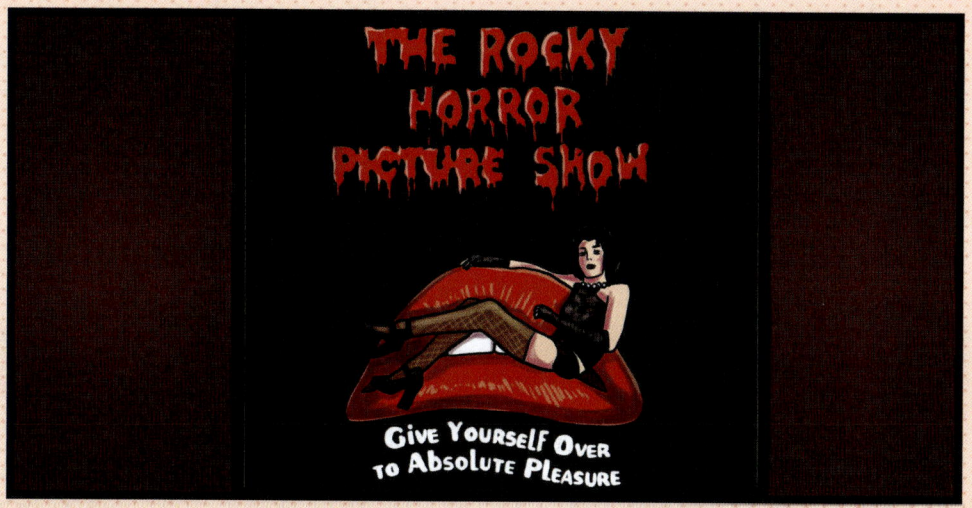

The majority of the audience would dress up as the characters, sing along with them, and mimic things that happened, such as spraying everyone with water when it rained and throwing actual toast at the screen when Frank-N-Furter raised a 'toast' at the infamous and ill-timed dinner scene. (Our group never dressed up or brought items to throw—I think that was because doing so, especially the dress-up part, would have been frowned upon by our families.)

There was intense expression of sexualities, making it clear heterosexuality is not the only sexual orientation. To me, and to some if not all of the others, *The Rocky Horror Picture Show* represented an affirmation of various forms of sexual identity—it was the complete opposite of what our families and the small town society represented. This was the first time we were exposed to a form of media that didn't depict queer characters in a negative way. It was such an amazing experience, and to those of us just learning about sexuality, the movie opened a door from our small, queer-phobic town to a world with no societal restrictions.

It was also an affirmation that whatever our sexual identity was turning out to be, it was okay and we weren't alone. In other words, being different was okay!

When we exited the theater at roughly two in the morning, we left with a feeling of youthful sexual freedom.

It is important to point out how we found out about this movie and the midnight showings. It was through Nate, who went for the first time with an older family member. Nate connected to the movie so strongly that when he felt the time was right, he took Kenji and me, and then the others, little by little until it became a weekend tradition. I didn't even know it existed until that first night we went. Once again, this larger-than-life sophomore was teaching this senior new things beyond our small town border.

I lost count of the number of times we saw the movie. If the other's couldn't make it, then Nate and I would go anyway. I don't have the words for how much fun it was!

I also want to mention how *Rocky Horror* affected me. Being a senior, and in my last year before I go out into the world as a queer man, the movie was such a breath of fresh air, given that until then I'd been exposed only to homophobic messages from my family and the community. It encouraged me to search for anything else I could relate to that might be out there past this small town. *Rocky Horror* was my starting point in life for being proud of who I am.

Our subgroup lived this cycle of partying, cruising, long phone conversations and *Rocky Horror* for the remainder of the school year. For me it was such a change from the three previous years of basically being invisible (by choice) until I could leave this small town and be whoever I was becoming. It gave me an unspoken freedom to be myself, be around great friends and enjoy crushing on Nate. It was something to look forward to every week, away from negative messaging from family and at school. It was a queer teen sanctuary. Then it all came to an abrupt halt…

CHAPTER 3
A1one

The subgroup, and all the fun that we had, was life-changing for me. However, there were times that Nate and I spent alone, and that's what I want to share with you now.

The long phone calls continued almost every night. The dune buggy rides into the mountains carried on and sometimes we just cruised in the Trans AM without everyone else.

We even had a little project together planting cannabis shoots, which started out in Nate's bedroom but had to be moved to my house which had a backyard shed with windows for light. None of the shoots grew past an inch, but we had fun trying.

Nate's mom saw the plants one day, and Nate being Nate, with his comical wit and fast thinking, told his mom that they were Algerian Mud Plants—and she seemed to believe it. We both got a big laugh out of it!

When my mom saw the plants I told her the same thing, but she gave me a very skeptical look.

We had fun, and I looked forward to those times with Nate. I always hoped he felt the same way. It was something just for us.

Occasionally when we were alone, Nate would start a wrestling contest over some small, light-hearted disagreement, and I always hoped this was just an excuse to touch me. At this point I still had no clear indication that he was crushing on me, so every touch brought me a sense of hope.

One afternoon at his house, the wrestling went a little farther than I would ever had imagined. Nate, who always had the upper hand in wrestling, abruptly pushed my face into his groin. I was shocked and scared at the same time. The scared boy in me took over and I immediately lifted my head, and we kind of just went on like it never happened. That was the first time that I felt that there was something between us, and that my crush wasn't one-sided.

After any partying, cruising or movie, I would drop everyone off at their house. I always dropped Nate off last—mainly to spend more time with him. One night towards the end of the school year, Nate asked if we could just sit in the car and talk.

I shut off the engine and asked him what was wrong—I could tell that something was off or different about him. He looked me straight in the eye and asked, "Why don't you touch me like you do with Kenji, Aiden, Christian and Luke?" (Note that he didn't mention Maya)

I was blown away! This was the second time I'd got a feeling that Nate felt more for me than just friendship. And in true Nate style, he went straight to talking about touching him! I was excited, but also scared, because my crush was slowly becoming something more—I believed.

So I asked Nate, "What are you talking about?"

He shared that he noticed that with the other boys, we'd hang on each other's arms and were close when sitting together, but with him I keep my distance. The fact that he was bringing this up, and so easily, was telling me that he liked me as more than just a friend, but I still didn't want to get my hopes up.

Well, Nate was right. I *was* doing that, and I knew why, but I didn't know how to tell him. It was different with the other boys in the group—I didn't have a crush on them. I felt that being to close to Nate, or touching him too much, would reveal that I was queer, and I didn't know (for sure) how he felt about that. In other words, I didn't want to come out with Nate unless I knew for sure that he was queer too. Therefore I'd felt it was best to have a crush on him from afar. I just didn't want to ruin our deep friendship and the subgroup.

So okay—how did I tell him about all this? I took a deep breath and said, "I know that I do that—its because I feel differently about you." I then extended my right hand (so nervous!) to take his. I knew that this would either go well, or would be the end of our friendship.

Nate put his hand in mine! We sat there in my car, just silent. I could feel that he was just as nervous as I was. Nervous and ecstatic at the same time. What a combination!

After about 10 minutes of holding hands, Nate said he'd go now and would call me in the morning. He did. That's how I knew that we were okay, and that the crush was mutual. Things entered a whole new level.

Before I go on, I need to give you a more extensive idea of what it was like to be queer in a small rural town in 1980-81, particularly in trying to find out about sex between two men.

Any teenager is nervous about their first few times, queer or straight. There was no internet or LGBTQIA+ positively inclusive shows or movies. No positive role models like Troye Sivan, Lil Nas X or Anderson Cooper. No queer sex discussions in school. There wasn't even a way to get queer porn easily. You couldn't ask or trust anyone, because it would out you into a very negative environment and any advise would be shame producing anyway. So you see, there is the initial nervousness, and then, for queer youth and even young adults, there is the fact that you are in the dark about sex. You feel unprepared in a whole different way—when the day comes.

For me personally, you then add the fact that it was hard for me to make any first moves for fear of being wrong about Nate and losing him and our friends, as well as being outed negatively. The fact that we had entered a new level of a relationship was scary—but exciting at the same time. A rollercoaster of emotions!

For a while after the hand-holding in the Trans AM, there was nothing more. The cruising and partying went on as usual, and neither Nate or I brought up that night again.

Then Nate asked me another favor. He asked me to drive him to his grandparents' house, which was about a four-hour drive from our small town. You won't be surprised to learn that I said yes! The selling point was that this road trip was only for Nate and me—and it was an overnight trip!

I kind of knew that Nate was most likely up to something, suggesting this trip—I assumed that it might even be sexual, or at least a chance to be close, away from our friends. I ended up being partially right.

Nate's grandparents didn't speak English well, so I wasn't able to easily communicate with them. They were so happy to see Nate, and despite the language barrier they made me feel welcome. Great Mexican food as well.

The night came. I was hoping that Nate and I would share a bedroom, and we did. Yes! Sex was not what I was looking for, mainly because, as I've said, nerves and lack of knowledge created an anxiety. Besides, we haven't even kissed yet. That is what I wanted—to kiss. It would be my first queer kiss and I wanted it to be with Nate. I hoped this would be the night.

The bedroom was set up with two twin beds. We were both nervous, but Nate seemed extra nervous. We stripped down to our baggy boxers—getting a corner-eye glance at each other—and then got into bed. About two minutes passed before Nate said he couldn't sleep.

REALLY! How could either of us sleep when we are alone in a room, wearing only baggy boxer shorts? Two teenagers crushing on each other with no idea on how to handle the crush.

Nate suggested we go outside on the patio to hang out, going through the window so as to not wake his grandparents. It was a great idea. The spring night was warm, and we sat together at a table (still in our baggy boxer shorts) and just talked like we did almost every night on the phone at home. Then we went to bed—in separate beds. This took all the anxiety of the moment and replaced it with one of the best nights of my young life, and I hope his too. We bonded even further that night. The next day we went to a rock concert, walked around the city and then drove home the next morning. After the trip we were closer, and less anxious.

It was getting close to my graduation, so Nate suggested a party with just the subgroup at my house since my parents and sister were going to be away for the weekend. Nate invited a classmate of his, Joaquin. We'd had teens outside of the subgroup join us before, but Nate was acting strange about inviting Joaquin. He was in that excited-but-nervous mode all week—and I later discovered why?

Joaquin was a nice guy, not popular, but well liked by most. Cute and straight, as far as I could tell.

The party was much the same as usual—drinking, pot, heavy metal music and just having a great time. As usual I didn't drink because I was the driver, and I wanted to make sure the house didn't get torn a part. Kenji installed a new window banner for the Trans AM in the middle of all the fun.

For some reason, Nate was intent on getting Joaquin drunk. It actually took very little to get Joaquin to that point.

It was a great party. Towards the end of the night, Kenji and Maya went off alone to another room to I assume have sex, or at least a heavy make-out session. Nate was sober, because as usual he had drunk or smoked only enough to feel good, so that he could lead the party. Christian, Luke and Joaquin were out of it.

When it was over, I began to drive them all home—or so I thought!

Joaquin was the second-to-last to be dropped off; Nate was always the last so I could spend as much time with him as possible. After we dropped off Joaquin (a longer drive than usual), I was shocked when Nate informed me that he'd told his parents he was spending the night at my house. I knew nothing about this, but (here we go again) I was excited and nervous, but I noticed it much less this time. All I could think was, *Is this going to be the night?* It was another opportunity for Nate and me to be alone in my house and to be close.

When we got home, I didn't go directly to the bedroom, but Nate did. He'd never spent the night before so I didn't know what his expectation was for where he'd sleep. I went into the bedroom to find Nate was in my bed (a waterbed, which was very popular in the early 80s). It was also dark. It was at that point that I knew something intimate was going to happen that night.

I stripped down to my baggy boxers and got into bed. At this point I remember being so frustratingly nervous, but also ready to intimately touch another guy who liked me back—in other words queer like me.

Then, in pure Nate style, he pulled out two blue boxer briefs (much shorter and tighter than what we were wearing) from under the covers and said, "Let's put these on!" I was like, "Okay, but where did you get these?"

We took off our underwear and put them on—all under the covers. As Nate was putting his on, he shared that he stole them from the store—crazy Nate!

I don't know what it was about those new short, tight

boxer briefs, but I went from frustratingly nervous to a mixture of horny, excited and nervous. I can only assume that Nate felt the same.

We lay there for about a minute—which seemed like a hour—until Nate started talking about touching again, like that night in the Trans AM. As he was talking, I remembered so clearly that Nate had been the one to initiate everything, and that I had been too scared. So as he was talking, I got up the courage to put my hand on his stomach.

OMG! Just the feel of his stomach gave me such a rush of ecstasy. What a beautiful feeling. I was in heaven. What came next was even more beautiful.

Nate placed his hand on mine and slowly moved it onto his dick. He was fully aroused! This was the first time that I felt an aroused guy, and it was amazing. The feeling that the guy you are crushing on feels the same sexually about you is beyond description. All those months of wondering if he was queer like me, and the would-we-hook-up someday question came to a close. Once my hand was on Nate's...we had sex.

This was a first time for both of us, so we went from beautiful to awkward and back to beautiful again. I remember thinking, how can something so beautiful and natural to me be the ridicule of straight people. It didn't add up. For me there was no doubt—I was a queer teen who was becoming a queer man, and I love it!

There was one freaky thing to me about having sex with Nate. He would not kiss. I tried a few times and he would freeze up. I didn't get it, because everything else was so amazing. I later learned that, to Nate, kissing would confirm that he is queer and that was not something he was ready to come to terms with.

As I begin to write this next part of my story, I feel the pain of what I'm about to share with you all over again. I have learned that this type of pain never really goes away in life. Instead, it's what you do in the aftermath that's important. This is the core reason I'm sharing my story with you.

After having my first queer sexual experience, I went to sleep very happy, and for the first time in a state of ecstasy.

When I woke up, my world changed. I turned to look at Nate, and saw him lying there with his eyes wide open, his body stiff, as if frozen. It seemed as if he hadn't been to sleep. It was even kind of creepy. I experienced a rush of anxiety—I just knew he was going to hurt me. I could feel it in my heart. I just didn't realize how bad it would be.

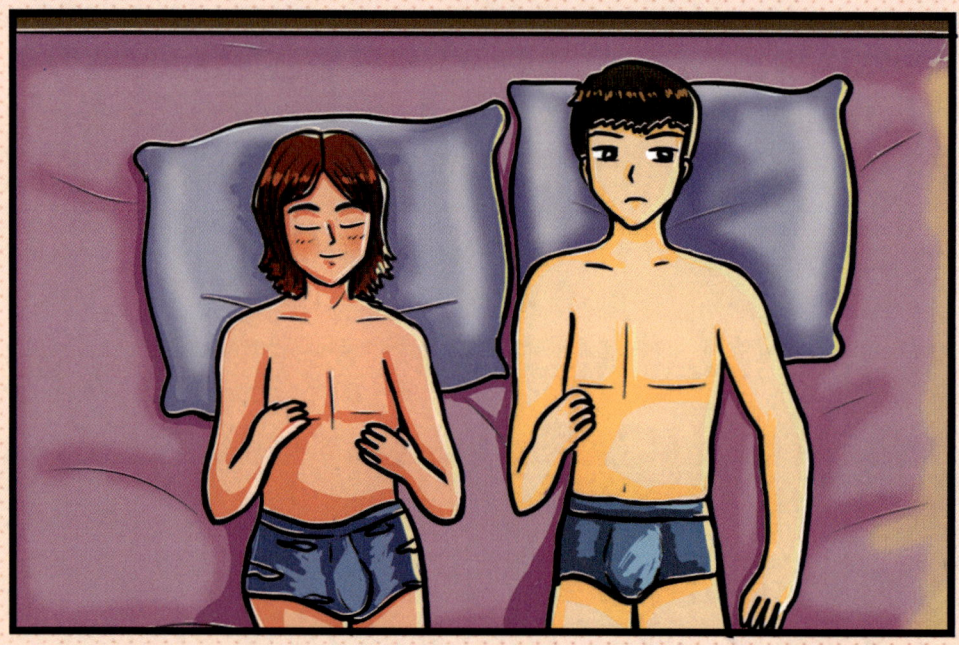

I kind of expected first-time awkwardness, but Nate took it to a whole different level. As I looked at him and said, "Good morning," he responded with a soft, "I need to go home." That was it. We got dressed and I drove him home. The entire time neither one of us said a word. I didn't want to say anything and I was scared of any negative response I would get.

We arrived at his house. He got out of the car, said nothing—not even goodbye—and closed the car door.

It was obvious to me that he regretted our encounter. I was so confused, hurt and confused again. I'm the type of person who (even to this day), when something like that happens, always wonders if I did something wrong. Along with the pain came confusion—I just couldn't think of anything that I had done to cause him to treat me that way. I knew he was younger than me, but he always was the initiator and I guess that confused me—but what came later that day was just cruel!

I decided to call Nate later that afternoon. All day I'd been dealing with hurt and was mystified about what happened, and by the afternoon I couldn't take it anymore. I drove to a pay phone, because my family was back and I didn't want to fight or appear sad in front of them (part of being in the closet-hide everything).

I dialed, the phone rang and I said, "It's me. Whats going on?"

Nate didn't even say hello back. He just started yelling. There was so much anger in his voice, served with a hint of cruelty.

I was so hurt! I just hung up on him. My whole body went numb. I felt like my heart cracked open.

How can something so special go so bad?

I cried so hard, ran to my car and sat there for the next 20 minutes, letting it all out. The pain was so bad I could barely breathe. The guy I liked, or even loved, had just rejected me in such a cruel and surprising way—I just wanted to die!

CHAPTER 4

The "Decision"

A day later, the pain inside me was so intense. I had lost the guy that I liked so much—and yes, for the first time I finally realized that I loved him. To lose the person that you love in such a cruel way was so much for me to process. And, it all came right before my graduation!

I made it through graduation. It was tough. Not being able to tell anyone in my family what was going on, because I was in the closet about my sexuality, was gut-wrenching, but I did an amazing job of hiding my pain.

The person I use to talk to now hated me with an undeserved vengeance. There was Maya, but I didn't know where anyone in the subgroup stood. So I kept it all inside until the night that changed my path forever.

It was toward the middle of June that I contemplated ending my life. I remember that night so clearly. The hurt was still inside me, just as strong as it was in the beginning. I saw no clear path to being happy in this small town, around all these people who made negative comments about queer people, and I *hated* the idea of living in the closet just to keep peace.

I also was sort of scared about being outed by Nate in a cruel way, but chances were low that he would do that because outing me would out him too, and neither one of us was ready for that fallout in a small rural town.

I felt I'd lost all my friends and I saw no future for myself. I felt alone and heartbroken. I just cannot describe the pain in words!

This is so hard to write about, but here it is.

I laid down on my waterbed, that same bed Nate and I had been intimate on, and decided to commit suicide.

In my bedroom I had several codeine pills left over from a dentist appointment. I took the prescription bottle from a drawer and stared at it. I needed water. I left my bedroom, and went into the kitchen and got the glass of water. My mom was in the kitchen and my sister was sitting at the dining room table—I'm not sure what she was doing. My dad wasn't home from work yet. I remember being so casual and so calm, considering the decision I had just made. I sauntered on past them like nothing unusual was going on.

I placed the glass of water on my nightstand, lay down and stared at the bottle of pills. I had no idea how many it took to die, but there were a lot of pills left so I felt it would get the job done. There was no internet in 1981 to look it up.

Then, something came over me as I stared at the pills. Something inside me asked (I know it sounds crazy), *Do you want to live and see what life has for you, or do you want to die?*

And, along with this internal question, it felt like a warm blanket was placed over me. I immediately got up and sat on the side of my bed, pill bottle and pills in hand, and answered the question: *I WANT TO LIVE! I WANT TO SEE WHAT I CAN BECOME IN LIFE!*

I got this amazing burst of energy and thought to myself, "If I live, what changes do I need to make? What I am experiencing in this town is not working."

I put the pills back in the bottle and the bottle back in the drawer, and went back to sitting on the side of my bed and thinking. So much was rushing through my mind, now that I had made the "decision."

Mentally, I made a list of what needed to change:

- I needed to move out of this small town and live in a place where I could be open about myself and happy as a queer man.

- I needed to go to college in this new place. The local college that I was planning to attend in the fall was no longer a healthy option.

- I needed to remove from my head all of the negative teachings from my family and the community about being queer. Those teachings were based on a lack of education, and biased and misguided religious ideas.

- I needed to find other people like me in a healthy way. Later I learned it was called a "queer community".

With this mental list (which, in hindsight, was pretty profound for someone my age), I went to the kitchen where my mom was washing dishes and said, "Mom, I've decided I'm moving to the city on September 1st."

She acknowledged my announcement with an "okay" or something similar. I knew she really didn't believe me at that time. I was young, and things can change—I'm sure that was what she was thinking. However, I was different. I was queer, and that alone was a driving force for change, growth, independence and success.

I learned through this experience that God had given me the gift of thinking things through before acting—which, by the way, has been life-long. I also for the first time felt a spiritual connection that I never learned in the Catholic church and the catechism (Catholic youth education) that I was raised with. I now realized that I was beginning my journey into adulthood and was becoming my own person, with my own thoughts and beliefs.

The next day I got in the Trans AM, drove to Tower Records, and bought a poster of the city skyline of San Francisco. I put it on my wall and it became the focal point of my goal for change for the next two and a half months.

After deciding to live, things fell into place. I kept a very low profile the next few days with the subgroup, not knowing what damage Nate had done or had not done. After all, they were Nate's classmates (except for Aiden) and I assumed their loyalty would reflect that. The decision paid off.

The first person in the group to call was Maya—of course. She was the only one who asked me straight out what was going on between Nate and me. I couldn't tell her the truth because outing Nate would have been wrong, and I wasn't ready to be outed as well. So I explained that it was simply a disagreement over something and I had no idea if it would fade away or be permanent. She seemed satisfied with that.

She explained that Nate was pressuring everyone in the group to not hang out with me anymore. No big reason, just don't do it. Maya went on to say that they were all confused, and they weren't going to do it. That turned out to be true. Then she said, "Let's do something!" We ended up making plans for *Rocky Horror* with some of the others.

The others began calling me as well. I shared with them my plans to move to the city on September 1st. It was welcomed with plans to hang out in the city from time to time, to party—youthful plans that would never come to fruition. For the rest of the summer, although in a different way, we had fun.

The subgroup and I hung out with the usual mix of partying, cruising and *Rocky Horror* for the next couple of months. The only missing part was Nate. We all seemed to just move on naturally. No one mentioned him and I didn't bring it up.

The hanging out became separate—one night I'd be cruising with Kenji and Luke, a few nights later I'd be hanging out in Tower Records with Maya and Christian. On the weekend, the large subgroup that had squeezed into the car had now dwindled to only one or two coming with me. Don't get me wrong, we still had a lot of fun. It was just that things were beginning to change.

Out of the blue, Maya shared with me that the group was hanging out with Nate too. She went on to say that Nate's constant put downs of me were getting on their nerves, so they started hanging out with him less. The result was that Nate made some new friends.

Even though the group was split, we all still had fun. But I felt a hole inside me with Nate's name attached to it. As time when on, I didn't hate Nate for what he did to me. I still had a strong crush (if not love) for him, and hoped things could change between us. I had no problem being just friends, but I didn't know what was going on in Nate's head, other than what Maya told me. The hurt of not being able to talk to anyone about this was immense. I had no one older than me that I could trust discussing a "queer" teen problem. This was one of the things in my life that I needed to change.

Towards the end of July, I got a call, again from Maya. She sounded very concerned. She said it was about Nate and asked if it was ok to discuss him with me. Of course I said yes—I still liked the guy.

Maya said that Nate has started making strange

comments to do with dying. They weren't suicidal in nature, but she felt it was Nate's weird style of expressing that he was unhappy. We knew each other so well, so I believed Maya.

She said that he was saying things, in his comedian-like style, such as, "I wonder if I died who would be at my funeral?" and, "Someone told me the other day that I'm too crazy and a daredevil, and that I have a death wish."

I said that knowing what I knew about Nate, it seemed he was thinking about his behavior; about being a daredevil and unsafe at times, and possibly about how he'd been treating me. She agreed.

That was the last serious phone conversation Maya and I had. What happened next overshadowed the last month of the summer!

The night of that phone conversation with Maya, Nate called me. I said hello and then listened to him, skeptical about why he was suddenly calling me—the person he told never to call him again. Could this be an apology and a new beginning? My heart was racing, because even though he hurt me so much, I still was crushing hard for him.

That was the night I learned that whatever your sexuality is, you cannot fight it. After some very small talk (but no apology), Nate said he wanted to hook up. You can guess what my answer was! That night he snuck over to my house, climbed into my bedroom via the window, and we were intimate. I was nervous, not because of Nate, but because my whole family was home. The next day I installed a lock on my bedroom door. It upset my dad, but I now needed privacy.

After that night we secretly hooked up either in my bedroom (via the window) or at a run-down motel by the freeway. I say secretly, because Nate made no suggestion that he and I should hang out publicly again, and I didn't suggest it either.

Intimacy with Nate was a mixture of teen nervousness on both sides, and cover-up. Maybe because I was older, I knew I was queer and was happy about it. Nate, on the other hand, had the feelings (obviously), but after intimacy, succeeded in making me feel bad again about being queer. He would talk about sex with girls; either girls he'd already fooled around with, or future conquests. This is not something you want to hear after being intimate.

The other negative was the fact that Nate would not kiss. Each time I attempted to kiss him, he pulled me back. For me, without kissing, the intimacy was empty—it all was just to get off. It made me feel so bad that eventually I made an excuse to not be available.

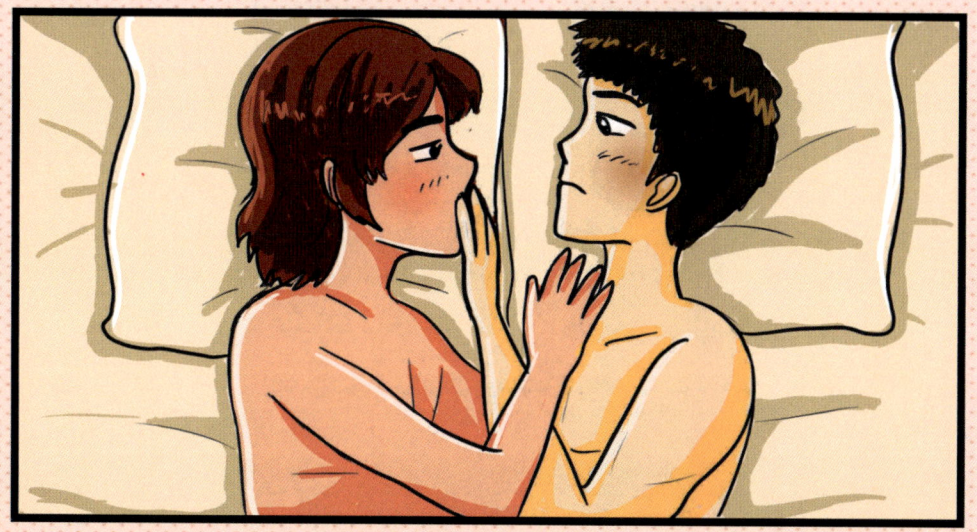

I liked Nate so much, but it was clear he couldn't offer what I wanted, and vice versa. Nate needed his processing time and I needed to move on and up. After making that excuse to not meet up, I never heard from Nate again. It was over.

I wasn't even upset this time around. The recent hook-ups were kind of like a closure for me. Nate would always be in my heart, and no matter how bad he hurt me, he also initiated self-growth in me. That crazy sophomore that had the boldness and guts to approach me that day forever changed my life—and for the better! I would never forget him. I also had no hard feelings—we were both young and in the process of finding ourselves. It was now time to get ready for the move to the city.

Like everything in life, things change. This time it was the subgroup, which began to fade away as well. Kenji and Maya no longer got along; Kenji moved on to another girl.

Christian and Luke found other friends in their junior year. However, after a year of flirting and being close, Luke and I finally made out! Not all the way, just made out—but it was amazing. Luke liked kissing, so that made me feel like there was hope in my future for something more than just getting off sexually. For the first time, Luke made me feel proud of liking other guys.

Aiden and his family moved away. Nate—well, that comes up later in the story. All of this separation made it much easier for me to begin my move to the city.

We had so much fun that last year; I'm forever grateful to all those friends. They brought a sense of inclusion, pride and acceptance that I hadn't had before. They would never know, but this mixture of sophomore, junior and a senior paved the way to my adulthood, from a self-isolated queer teen to a proud queer man. I only hope I contributed to something positive for them as well.

Making the "decision" to live and see what I could become became the best choice of my life. Things started turning around for the best—pretty much immediately after the decision. Now it was time to move on and up to the next chapter of my life! (Note: The story of Nate and me is not over.)

CHAPTER 5

More
Summer 1981

Along with events in the diminishing subgroup, that summer other things happened that positively effected my independence and development as a young queer male.

My mom asked me to work at my parents' restaurant and bar helping out as needed. I worked along side her as she showed me the ropes of the business. The clientele was interesting. I had the opening three-hour shift, from 11am-1pm. With that, I saw the chronic alcoholics of the small town waiting in their cars for me to open the door. Then around 1145am came the town's business owners, bankers, and so on, for a drink and lunch. I thought that I'd hate the job, but it ended up being fun.

Around the end of June I took a three-hour drive by myself to what I'd heard was a liberal college town. (It would become my passion to explore the world outside of the small town.) I was not disappointed. I just wanted to explore. I walked around the college and the nearby stores, and immediately saw the difference in the people, from the way they dressed to an atmosphere of diversity. I loved it!

I came across a jewelry store for young women that advertised ear-piercings with a free ear stud. Caught up in the ambiance of the liberal surroundings, I got up the courage to get a gold stud pierced in my left ear.

Needless to say it did not go over well when I got home. I

was ordered by my mom to take it out, but I didn't. I explained that I liked it and that what people thought wasn't important to me. It was the first time that I said no to my mom; you should have seen her face. My independence and queer development was starting to form.

The second thing that I learned during my trip to the college town was that there was a straight bar that changed clientele to queer on Fridays. I saw this on a posted flyer in a store, and took it with me.

Once in July and another time in August, I drove the three hours at night to this club and back again, getting home around 3am. Each time my parents didn't even notice—or they stayed silent—I think it was the first.

I cannot adequately express the sense of freedom, the experience of seeing a crowded club full of people like me for the first time—with a sea of cute guys! The music blended deep inside me. I even remember the song that was playing the first time that I walked in: "You Make Me Feel (Mighty Real)," by Sylvester. This was the beginning of my conversion from heavy metal to modern rock/dance/new wave music (as it was called in the 80s).

This was a 21-and-over-club, but no one was carding at the door. They carded as you bought a drink, so it was no problem for me getting in because I was driving. Not drinking and driving was important to me, because I had a close aunt and uncle who were killed by a drunk driver when I was 16, and I vowed never to drive under the influence of anything. That has held true all of my life, and it's why I never minded being the designated driver with Nate and the subgroup.

The most impressionable experience that summer began while I was working at the restaurant. There was a cute businessman (he said he was 32) who came in every day before lunch, had food and a drink, and I assume went back to work. One afternoon when I was getting ready to finish my shift (he was the only one left at the bar), he just came out and asked if I would hook-up with him (a very bold move!). I was stunned, and there went the nerves again. I had only been with Nate. I wanted to, so—very nervously—I said yes. We hooked up that night. I'm pretty sure it was my new earring that signaled to him it was somewhat safe to ask me. In 1981 a man wearing an earring wrongly meant to straight people that he was queer.

Boy! He was really taking a chance, asking someone for a queer hook-up in a homophobic small town. I later asked him what gave him the courage. He said he always had a feeling I was gay, but the earring and his attraction to me gave him the courage to ask me. I'm glad that he did, because it became a life-confirming and life-changing experience that affected my adulthood from that point forward.

We met that night in a motel in another small town close by. This businessman taught me that night how beautiful queer sex was, and how to be passionate. This experience was so important, because all of my life I have heard nothing but negativity toward queer sex. First with Nate and now with this small-town businessman, I now knew all that negativity was wrong. Queer sex is a beautiful thing.

We never met up again. I actually never saw him again. The businessman didn't come back to the restaurant during my shift. I found out later, casually and unknowingly, from my mom, that he came in at night with—his wife and infant child!

What the fuck? Another learning experience for me. This cute 32-year-old man who taught me the beauty and passion of male-to-male sex was living a lie. His way to survive in this small homophobic town was to marry, have a child and publicly present himself as being completely heterosexual, but secretly have sex with men.

I was stunned, and my mom didn't even realize what she was telling me. I remember thinking, I never want to be like that. It is so critical to be your true self. I was so disappointed in him. How unfair to his family and to himself. It gave me more incentive for my move to the city.

That summer-of-1981 experience connected the end of the subgroup with my development as a queer man, and to moving on and up to be my true self.

CHAPTER 6
Moving On

A first crush/love stays within your heart forever—at least, that's my experience. As I got ready to begin my adult life in the city, Nate was always in my thoughts—even today as I write my story. Please remember this as I write on.

September 1st had arrived! The night before, I packed up all my belongings that were mobile: clothes and more clothes, a small LED clock radio for music, and my cassette tapes. I put everything in a large box and stuffed it into the back seat of the Trans AM. That seat, once loaded with friends rocking out to heavy metal music or the soundtrack of *Rocky Horror*, was now serving as a moving van.

The hardest part about leaving was saying goodbye to my mom. She and I were close. It was extremely hard for her to see my announcement in June becoming a reality in September. Crying, she handed me some money to get my new life started, hugged me hard and ran into the house. I pulled out of the driveway, didn't look back, and began what was a three-day journey.

I chose San Francisco firstly because it was a beacon of LGBTQIA+ freedom and I felt I could be myself there, and secondly because I had an aunt and cousin in the city who allowed me to stay with them while I got settled. Also, I'd started making new friends from a classified ad I saw in a magazine that I bought at Tower Records (more about this later) and some of the contacts were from the city. It seemed like a great place to start.

I had mentioned to a new friend of mine, who was from San Jose, CA, that I really liked working with kids. She told me about her job working with children in the South Bay at a military base, and that the base in San Francisco was hiring. A week later I gained employment as a preschool teacher's aide, and loved it. Kids have such a way of placing life into perspective, with the way they think. This job led to college and eventually a 37-year career. I am retired now and have the time to write—something I've dreamed about doing since the 90s.

The following year I enrolled in the city's community college, which led me to completing undergraduate studies and on to graduate school. This educational path eventually led me to entering the world of senior administration of Child & Youth Services for the military. I was accepted at a state university closer to the small rural town where I grew up, but that would have been a negative situation for me as a queer man, so I started at the community college level in the city and kept learning, developing and leading others to make our programs high quality for children and youth.

College and a number of life experiences began to teach me, along with how to be myself, that those conservative messages I was taught either from my family or in that rural town did not fit into "real life." I began to learn and witness very clearly that heteronormative messaging, the idea that you must follow a certain script in life according to your birth gender and that you have to "go with the flow", as my mom use to say (this drove me crazy), was false. It was the product of a lack of knowledge and misleading, hateful religion. I love my family, both extended and immediate, but that does not mean I love their negative messaging. It is what I had to get away from—and did—and it shifted my life path in a positive direction.

I started meeting other guys, first through a classified magazine ad (there was no internet in 1981-82) that helped queer people meet other queer people. We would write letters back and forth, getting to know each other, and then if things go well, would meet in person. It was kind of fun! This method was actually amazing. I met some guys from around the San Francisco Bay Area and even made a couple new queer friends.

The other way I met guys was the 18 and over gay clubs (no alcohol). A few clubs in the city had them, and, as is the case for all queer people when they walk into a gay club for the first few times, I felt like I was home. It was amazing to be around people like me! I looked forward to clubbing every weekend.

The final step was getting my first apartment. I had to live simply because I was in college and paying for that, but I was blessed to have my job, and it was so much better being completely independent and living my true self. I now had a place for my beloved sound system as well, and a beautiful view of the city. In the back of my heart, I hoped that Nate would join me someday. I could help him get settled in the city. I guess that was only natural to feel.

This chapter is important to my story, because I want to share the key events that happened to me after thinking hard about whether to live or die. Not everything was easy, in fact most of it was hard, but it's important to see what you can become after you let go of any negative forces holding you back, or feeling bad about yourself because you are queer.

I did, of course, go back to visit my family periodically—holidays, etc. I even made an impromptu visit when a guy I was dating a few years later turned out to be a bad person. I just wanted to be by my mom. She could tell that I was upset about something, but I never let on why. It was great to eat her home-cooking and see the family. When I visited I laid low in the town. Yes, there were negative queer-phobic comments every time I visited, but I just ignored it. However, I started to get the nerve to speak up later on.

I never contacted anyone from the subgroup when I visited. I just felt like it was past history and we'd all moved on. My life now was work-college-clubs. I am so happy that I made the decision to live life.

CHAPTER 7
The Death

The following summer, I was taking classes to finish my associates degree in child development, clubbing on the weekends and of course working during the week. I was living paycheck to paycheck, but it was worth it because I was in complete control of my life. Once again, I was so happy that I'd chosen to live my life and see what I could become.

One afternoon, I came back to my apartment after buying groceries for the night. One of my San Francisco favorites—sourdough bread—was top of the list to prepare. As I was slicing the bread, I cut my thumb with the knife. I don't know what made me instinctively do this, but I immediately looked at the clock, which read 05:05pm. I cleaned myself up, bandaged my thumb, threw the bloodstained part of the bread away and continued making my dinner that late afternoon.

The next evening my mom called. She began by asking how I was doing, and so on. Then she said, "You know that friend you had? His name was Nate?"

"Yeah?" I said, wondering why she was bringing him up.

"I wanted to tell you that he died yesterday—I don't know if you heard."

You can imagine my heart and whole body just going numb.

Mom shared what she had heard through small-town gossip, that it was some kind of accident. When she was told the name of the "high schooler" she remembered that Nate was a friend of mine.

I politely went on with the phone call, but I remember nothing that was said after the news about Nate—it just didn't seem real. My mom said she'd call tomorrow and read me the local newspaper clipping, which would have more details.

I sat in a chair overlooking the city skyline and just stared out the window. I was hollow inside for days, weeks, and eventually years.

As she'd promised, mom called with more details. I'm going to share with you what I know, as well as my thoughts around those details. Why? Obituaries don't always share the "whole" person's story when it comes to the queer community (especially someone in the questioning stage and so young). In the 1980s (AIDS epidemic era), a lot families lied about how their family member died. What I'm trying to say is that there is the published obituary, and then there's the behind-the-story of the individual. I will write about both.

The obituary stated that Nate's death was accidental. He'd gone hiking with some friends (all new friends I didn't know), taken an unrecommended route, slipped and fallen to his death. As all obituaries do, it listed Nate's likes and funeral service schedule.

The one detail that stood out to me from the local newspaper report was the time that Nate died. It was 05:05pm—*the exact time I had cut my thumb!*

This was unbelievable. I truly felt then, and still feel today, that when you are so close to someone emotionally, you seem to get a message from a higher power than yourself that something is wrong. You hear people talk about this sort of thing all the time. I feel that it was God letting me know that Nate (the guy I still loved) was gone. God had me look at the clock when I got the cut to mark the time.

This was also the time that I realized as a young adult that God does not hate queer people. He loves us just the same. All that hate rhetoric from unbridled organized religion was wrong. I could feel it inside me.

I kept remembering all of the fun Nate and I had and how, I will say it again, that bold and gutsy sophomore (who died before he became a senior) entered my isolated life and influenced it, through the good and the bad. I dusted off the AC/DC cassette tape and *Rocky Horror* soundtrack (I was into new wave now) and sat and reminisced in his honor. At the same time I was trying to decide if I should go to the funeral service. With much thought and hesitation, I decided to go.

I traveled back to the town I grew up in and went to the funeral to say good-bye to Nate. What was to come caught me by yet another queer-phobic surprise.

I borrowed my mom's car and drove to the funeral by myself. Once again, I decided to not contact any of the subgroup. It was possible I would see some of them there—I didn't know.

It was rough. I sat at the back of the church. I didn't recognize anyone except the family in the front.

Nate's casket was closed with a large blow-up picture of him surrounded with flowers. It was so hard to see that. It made all of this real. It wasn't a dream—Nate was gone.

It was a normal Catholic service. I remember thinking that if Nate were there he would have thought, this is boring, so let's go do something fun.

The one thing during the funeral that hit me wrong was the mention that his girlfriend was sitting with the family. What? I guess it could have been so—or had Nate been covering up or in denial about his sexuality, like he did with me? It had been quite a while since I was in contact with Nate, so maybe it was true? I just felt like this funeral didn't reflect the Nate that I knew.

I wasn't planning to go to the reception, but I bumped into someone who talked me into it. From the moment I walked in

I could sense I wasn't welcome. I tried to give condolences to Nate's family but was distracted by friends of the family who led me away from them. After that happened, I left. I was already deep in mourning for Nate and then that happened—it really pissed me off!

As I was walking to the car, I was hailed by Maya! It was so great to see her. I was hoping for a friendly face and there she was. I needed that after what happened. We sat in my mom's car and caught up on our lives. Maya wasn't in contact with anyone in the subgroup. She did see Kenji and Christian at the service, sitting in the front, but I didn't see them.

Then we had a deep conversation about Nate. Maya asked, "Do you think that he did this on purpose, or even subconsciously? All that talk about wondering who would be at his funeral and the daredevil in him—I just wonder?"

I said, "I am kind of glad you brought this up. It crossed my mind as well. I have to believe it was accidental, but what I know about Nate and how young he was concerns me. Maya, we will never know."

That was the last time I ever saw Maya.

Then like in any small rural town, I bumped into Kenji's mom at the local convenience store. I really liked her. She was a youthful mom and if anyone knew anything in the town, it was her. She asked me to go to her house and chat for a while. I did. I didn't see Kenji.

After catching up and small talk, she opened up about a situation with Nate and Kenji. She shared that Kenji recently told her he felt Nate had made a sexual advance towards him, and didn't know what to do about it.

According to Kenji's mom, Nate unexpectedly stayed overnight one time. While in Kenji's bed (a queen bed) something happened (a touch or comment—I don't know) that gave Kenji the impression that Nate was advancing sexually. Oddly, it was the same pattern as the night Nate and I were first intimate. Impromptu sleepover, and you know the rest.

I felt comfortable with Kenji's mom, and told her I was queer (gay was the word that I used at the time). This led to more conversation. I also shared how unwelcome and shunned I felt at the reception—it was still bothering me.

Like I said, if anyone had the scoop on town happenings, it was Kenji's mom. She told me she kind of had an idea why I was shunned at the reception. Apparently, back when the subgroup and I were hanging out, my dad and Nate's mom met to discuss concerns regarding our friendship. That's all she knew.

Also around the same time, my dad bumped into Kenji's mom at some kind of town function and brought up his concerns to include that fact that he suspected that I might be gay—but never wanted to know for sure. We thought he may have said the same thing to Nate's mom.

That all made sense! I was being shunned because I represented a ridiculous and homophobic portal to queerness and it was best to eradicate me. It didn't matter at all that I cared so deeply for Nate. It didn't matter that I was a major part of his very short life. It didn't matter that I was putting myself through college and had established a career. It didn't matter that I was a good person. It only mattered that any hint of queerness regarding Nate be hidden and erased.

I appreciated the heart-to-heart talk with Kenji's mom, but just wanted to get back to the city! These people wanted to hide everything and assign it to gossip. I was *done!* I traveled back as soon as I could, away from this negative environment, and moved on and up.

Nate didn't get to move on, though. He would have started his senior year. He had time to figure out who he was because he was young, but now that was gone. Nate had limitations in a queer-phobic rural town. I know because I lived it.

CHAPTER 8

First Crush
to Life

Deep in my heart, I'd been hoping Nate would graduate, then possibly move to the same city as me. I could help him get settled. He could live his true and whole self, even if that meant we would only be friends—which was the likely outcome.

Contrary to anyone else's opinion in that small rural town, Nate and I had a connection. That became very clear when I cut my thumb. I was made aware that something in my life, or someone especially close to me, was experiencing something negative. I didn't know it at the time, but it later became clear. I also believe that a higher power was the messenger.

Nate was my first crush and that means everything. To this day he has a strong presence in my life and will never leave my heart. It is enough to inspire me to write my story. You never forget your first crush! And if it includes intimacy, then it is really embedded in your memories. In my case, the crushing was fun and exciting and made me feel alive. It was an introduction to my queer self. Nate's response to intimacy led me, via a lot of pain, to learn that life goes on and it is critical to not take your life away. See what you can become!

I want to end my story with concepts that led me to a fulfilling, amazing life as a queer man in a homophobic society.

You have to remove yourself from any negative environment. This process will be different for each individual. Remaining in a queer-phobic environment can only lead to a negative path. You can always go back, once you're educated and more prepared, to address queer phobia—if it is safe to do so.

You have to find a path to education. It could be college or something else. You have to think for yourself, not just listen to others and "go with the flow."

Read. Find books on queer history, queer memoirs, queer fiction, queer non-fiction and life. You can also take online queer history courses. You will learn that you are not alone—past and present.

Watch. There are a lot of indie and mainstream movies and shows that depict all of us in a more positive light these days. You/we are not alone!

Act. When ready, you can express your queer self in a variety of ways such as art, writing, film, education, advocacy…the list goes on. Do what is inside you and remember as you live life, someone younger is watching and getting motivated to live their queer life.

Vote. The power to vote for people who will support our queer community is critical! Voting equals power. Not voting gives the power to the queer-phobic community.

It's important to find a path to improving the way of life for queer adults, children and/or youth. Now and for future generations.

You have to replace all of the negative messaging about queer people that you have heard from school, family, friends, religion and negative politics, with the truth. This comes as you follow the previous suggestions.

If you are contemplating hurting yourself, or even suicide, like I did, please take a big breath, pause and ask yourself, *"Do I want to live and see what I can become?"* Hopefully the answers is yes!

I chose yes and I have experienced an amazing queer life. I have seen the world as a queer traveler. I have met and remain friends with other queer people from all over the world. What I am saying is, choose life! Get away from the negative! MOVE ON & UP! If you still have doubts please speak to someone!

LGBTQIA+ Friendly
Hotlines

(www.thetrevorproject.org)
1-866-488-7386

LGBT National Hotline
1-888-843-4564

When I was writing this story, I came across a movie made in Argentina about queer teen suicide. It was based in the 90s. During and after the film I thought, wow, it doesn't matter which decade you came of age in, our stories are the same—even in the 2020s and beyond.

It is critical to share these queer stories of self-harm and confusion so that others will make the decision to live. The community in this movie (which was a true story) lost two queer teens to suicide. The first couldn't get past a boyfriend rejection, and the second suffered from confusion of identity. Neither had any support system—just community queer phobia.

Nate's story was different. I do know that Nate struggled with his sexuality, but that's all I know. However, he died too. Nate never got to develop his true self like I did, and I hate that so much!

I began this story by emphasizing the negative queer-phobic messaging that can come from elementary school (when young children begin to feel different, but don't know why) to the pre-teen and teen years in which the question of why begins to emerge with a person's sexuality. A queer child or youth are usually surrounded by queer-phobic messaging—messaging that they have to overcome. Some make it through, some do not. And that has to stop!

I knew early on that I didn't want to "fake it", but coming out in the small town might have led to my death. Instead, I chose invisibility. This is why I didn't go to dances, proms or sports events. I would of had to fake it, and I wasn't willing to do that.

Everything changed when I met Nate, Kenji, Maya, Christian, Luke and Aiden. They participated in dances and sports, but recognized early in their life that there are different people out there with different interests. Lucky for me, they allowed me to be myself and enter their subgroup.

Being a part of the group led me to my first queer sexual experience and a greater emergence of self and pride.

Heartache and pain let me know that I needed to move on with my life as I watched Nate's struggle and confusion, small town queer phobia and a lack of queer community for support.

Once I moved on, a new excitement of wanting to meet hot new guys, go to college and just living life as a queer man emerged!

When I drove my Trans AM over the Oakland/San Francisco Bay Bridge in September of 1981, all of those dreams began to come true. It was not easy (downright hard at times), but through education and hard work, it became easier each year. It is my hope for all queer teens and young adults to experience the same and find their path...

ACROSS THE BRIDGE
(whatever and wherever your bridge may be)

ALSO by Michael Simones

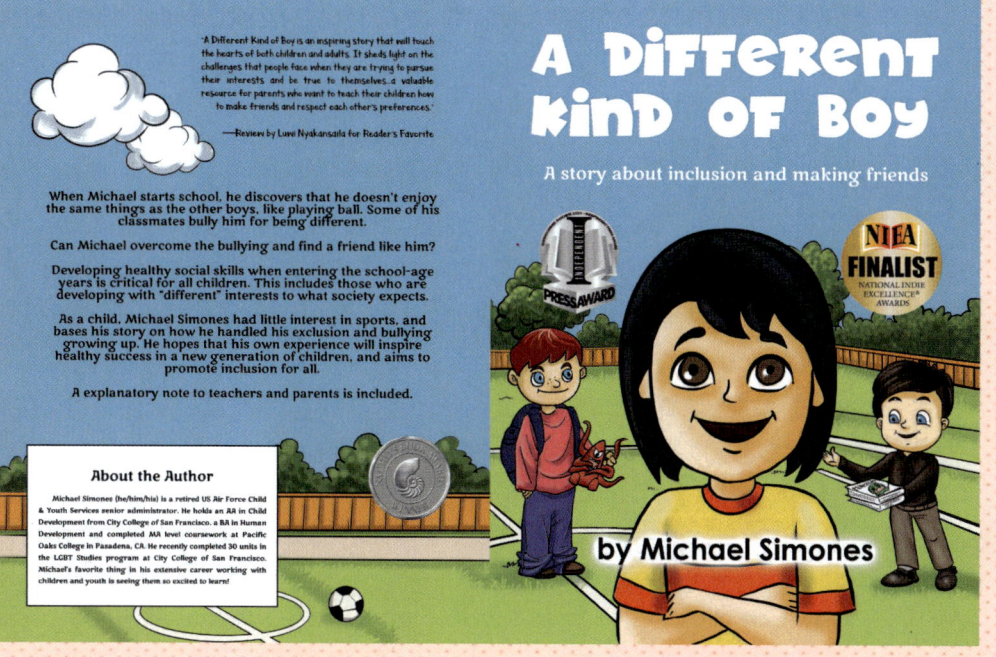

"A Different Kind of Boy is an inspiring story that will touch the hearts of both children and adults. It sheds light on the challenges that people face when they are trying to pursue their interests and be true to themselves, a valuable resource for parents who want to teach their children how to make friends and respect each other's preferences."

—Review by Lunei Nyakansaila for Reader's Favorite

When Michael starts school, he discovers that he doesn't enjoy the same things as the other boys, like playing ball. Some of his classmates bully him for being different.

Can Michael overcome the bullying and find a friend like him?

Developing healthy social skills when entering the school-age years is critical for all children. This includes those who are developing with "different" interests to what society expects.

As a child, Michael Simones had little interest in sports, and bases his story on how he handled his exclusion and bullying growing up. He hopes that his own experience will inspire healthy success in a new generation of children, and aims to promote inclusion for all.

A explanatory note to teachers and parents is included.

About the Author

Michael Simones (he/him/his) is a retired US Air Force Child & Youth Services senior administrator. He holds an AA in Child Development from City College of San Francisco, a BA in Human Development and completed MA level coursework at Pacific Oaks College in Pasadena, CA. He recently completed 30 units in the LGBT Studies program at City College of San Francisco. Michael's favorite thing in his extensive career working with children and youth is seeing them so excited to learn!

A DIFFERENT KIND OF BOY

A story about inclusion and making friends

NIEA FINALIST
NATIONAL INDIE EXCELLENCE® AWARDS

by Michael Simones

ABOUT THE AUTHOR

Michael Simones is a retired Air Force Child & Youth Services senior administrator, and award-winning author. He holds an AA in Child Development, BA in Human Development and has completed MA coursework in Human Development. In 2021 he completed 30 units of LGBT Studies as well. During his 37 years of service to military families, Mr. Simones taught preschool children for 10 years, then served as a Curriculum Specialist and Child Development Center Director. He entered senior administration the last 10 years of service as a Child and Youth Civilian Commander at Air Force programs all over the world. Throughout his career Mr. Simones has been awarded citations from the US Air Force to include the 2015 Air Force Child & Youth Services Commander of the Year. Mr. Simones resides in San Francisco, CA.

In retirement, Mr. Simones writes books for children, youth and young adults that support positive social and self-esteem affirmation and inclusion—especially for those who are bullied and emotionally abused because of who they naturally are. Mr. Simones' vision is to write books that inspire children and youth that feel different, to be who they are naturally and create a thriving life that overcomes negative messaging from home, school and the playground.

Made in the USA
Las Vegas, NV
13 January 2026

36160058R00076

As a queer teen in a small American town in the 1980s, Ryder purposely stays in the shadows. At high school he meets friends, including his first crush, Nate, who unconsciously showed him a road to being proud of who he is. A pride that stays with him for life. But growing up in this small, queer-phobic town wasn't easy, and along the way Ryder will battle to overcome thoughts of suicide. Queer youth (no matter what the decade) have to deal with high school heteronormative expectations that do not match who they are. How did Ryder, Nate and friends break this barrier?

In *Across the Bridge*, Ryder graphically and directly shares his queer coming-of-age story in the hope that it will inspire new generations of queer youth and young adults to thrive and not give into queer oppression.

This book is meant to be a quick read for all, but especially for queer youth contemplating suicide.

ISBN 9798987731024

9 798987 731024

90000